Bacon's Rebellion

1676

Thomas J. Wertenbaker

CLEARFIELD

Originally published
1957

Reprinted for
Clearfield Company by
Genealogical Publishing Co.
Baltimore, Maryland
1993, 1994, 1998, 2001, 2007

ISBN-13: 978-0-8063-4798-1
ISBN-10: 0-8063-4798-8

Made in the United States of America

*Jamestown 350th Anniversary Historical Booklet
Number 8*

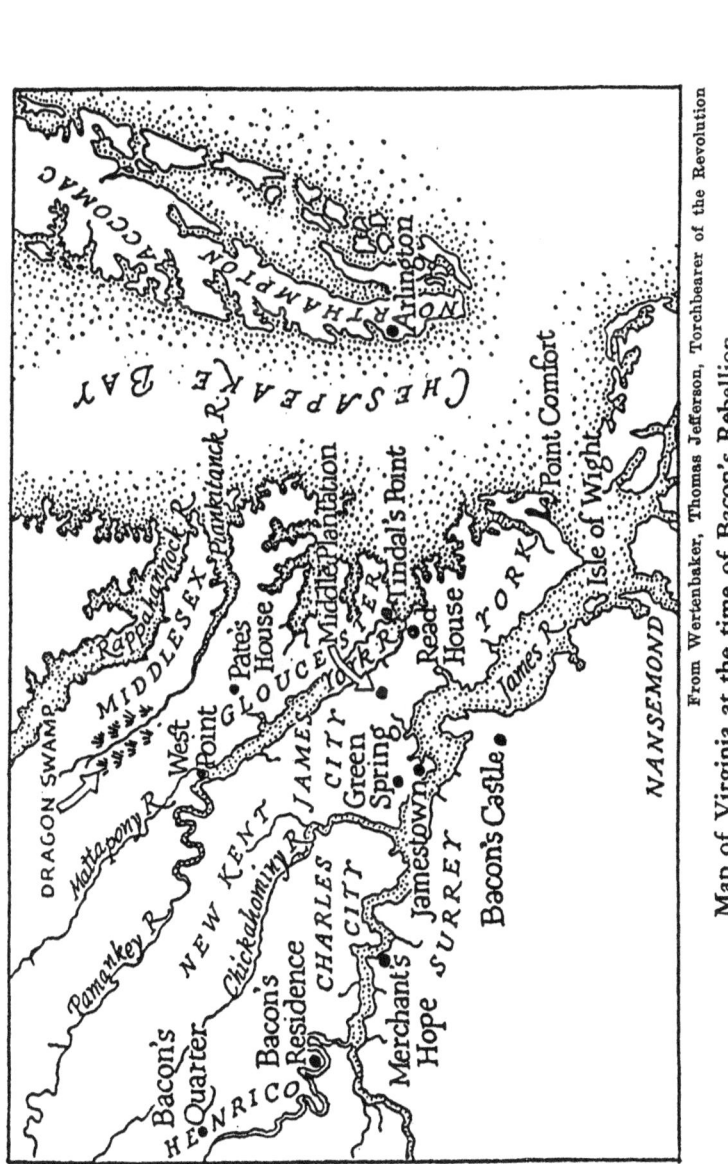

Map of Virginia at the time of Bacon's Rebellion

From Wertenbaker, Thomas Jefferson, Torchbearer of the Revolution

BACON'S REBELLION, 1676

The months just preceding the year 1676 were marked in Virginia by ominous signs of disaster. A great comet streamed through the sky "like a horsetail," and it was well known that that meant pestilence or war. Then came tens of thousands of pigeons, stretching across the sky as far as the eye could see. They were followed by vast swarms of what seem to have been cicadas, which rose out of the ground, ate the fresh leaves of the trees, and then disappeared. So those who believed in omens were not surprised when the year was marked by the greatest catastrophe in the history of the colony.

But to understand what happened it is necesssary to go back thirty-five years to the appointment by Charles I of Sir William Berkeley as Governor of Virginia. No doubt the King considered this an especial act of grace to the colony, for Berkeley was a member of the Privy Chamber, and as such lived in the royal palace. It was this, perhaps, which fired him with an intense loyalty for the House of Stuart which endured to the day of his death. To dispute the omnipotence of the king was in his eyes the darkest of crimes. A Master of Arts at Oxford, a writer of some merit, polished in manner, he seemed out of place in the forests of Virginia. Perhaps it was his passion to rule which brought him to the colony, perhaps it was cupidity, for he accumulated there a fortune of considerable size.

He had been in Virginia but a few months when word reached him of the outbreak of the Civil War in England. He must have been horrified that anyone should dare to take up arms against the sacred person of the King, and he sought permission to return to England to defend him. So, in the summer of 1644, when Charles was bearing down on the Parliamentary forces under Essex in Cornwall, Berkeley was with him. And he looked on with deep satisfaction as Sir Richard Grenville ransacked Lord Roberts' house at Lanhydrock, eight miles north of Fowey, and made off with silver plate worth £2000.

It was probably soon after this that word came of the terrible Indian massacre of April 18, 1644, for Berkeley was back in Virginia on June 7, 1645. Placing himself at the head of the forces which had been bringing fire and destruction to the Indian villages, he soon forced the savages to seek refuge in the woods and swamps. After he had captured their aged chief Opechancanough, they sued for peace.

Upon receiving news of the execution of Charles I, Sir William proclaimed Charles II King. And when, in 1652, a Parliamentary fleet sailed up the James to reduce the colony, he summoned the militia and prepared for a stubborn resistance. It was only when his Council pointed out the folly of defying the might of Britain that he reluctantly agreed to surrender. But his soul was filled with bitterness. So, with the restoration of Charles II to the throne, when once more he was governor of Virginia, he was determined to permit no more of representative government than his commission and instructions made necessary.

This he did by corrupting the Burgesses and continuing them by prorogations for many years. He took on himself "the sole nominating" of all civil and military officers, picking out such persons as he thought would further his designs. Collectors', sheriffs', justices' places were handed out to the Burgesses with a lavish hand. The list of Burgesses in the so-called Long Assembly sounds like a military roll call, for of the thirty members in 1666, six were colonels of militia, two lieutenant-colonels, one a major, and fourteen captains. Philip Alexander Bruce states that "a large proportion of the justices were also members of the House of Burgesses." In this way he "gained upon and obliged" the "men of parts and estates" in the Burgesses, and made them subservient to his will. "He has so fortified his power over us as of himself without respect to our laws to do what so ever he pleased," it was said.

Sir William further bound his favorites to him by granting them great tracts of the best land. "Some take up 2,000 acres, some 3,000, and others 10,000, and many more have taken up 30,000." They cultivated only a fraction or perhaps not any of these great tracts, merely putting up "a hog house to save the lapse." So when newcomers looked around for land, they were faced with the alternative of becoming tenants or of taking up "remote barren lands" on the frontiers.

The poor planters complained bitterly of the great sums voted by the Assembly for their own salaries, those of certain officers, and for various other expenses. In 1675 the Speaker of the House received 15,000 pounds of tobacco, the clerk 15,000. The total cost of this session was 539,390 pounds of tobacco, that of the session of February, 1676, 616,652 pounds. When the salary of collectors was added the total was 1,601,046 pounds, or perhaps an average of 150 pounds for every family.

The people were convinced that the heavy taxes served no other purpose than to enrich Berkeley's favorites. "Consider their sudden advancement," said Bacon. "See what sponges have sucked up the public wealth, and whether it hath not been privately contrived away by unworthy favorites, by vile juggling parasites, whose tottering fortunes have been repaired and supported." And it was obvious that Berkeley himself had taken care to get the largest share of the plunder. At the outbreak of Bacon's Rebellion he owned the plantation at Green Spring, five houses in Jamestown, four hundred cattle, several hundred sheep, sixty horses, "near £1,000 worth of wheat, barley, oates, and corn," and some valuable plate.

Part of this fortune came to him through a monopoly of the beaver trade with the Indians. He seems to have cashed in on this by licensing the traders on the frontier and taking a large part of their profits. Though he had trouble in collecting his dues, he received each year several hundred pounds of beaver fur. His obedient Assembly added to his wealth by voting him money from time to time. This they excused to the indigent tax payers as due him for what he had laid out in "beneficial designs." But the poor planter, in his rags, leaning on his hoe in his little tobacco patch, secretly cursed as Lady Berkeley drove past in her coach.

The people complained bitterly that they had been cheated of the right to govern themselves. That no power whatsoever should tax them without their own consent was the basic principle of English liberty. Yet it was but a mockery to contend that men who had sold themselves to the governor and whom they were given no opportunity to oust from office, were their true representatives in voting away their money.

In local government Sir William was supreme. He it was who appointed the sheriffs and the justices of the peace who, as members of the county courts, had judicial, legislative, and executive powers. The county tax was usually larger than that laid by the Assembly, for it had to cover the salaries of the Burgesses, the cost of building courthouses, prisons, and bridges, and of killing wolves, etc. When the justices in levying taxes retired to a private room and locked the door, there was grave suspicion of fraud. Is it not obvious, men said, that they do not tell us what the taxes are for, because part of the money they put in their own pockets?

Much of the money wrung from the taxpayers was squandered upon foolish projects. In 1662, at the advice of the King, the Assembly voted to build thirty-two brick houses at Jamestown, and levied thirty pounds of tobacco per poll to pay for them. Since the mere erection of houses when there was no need for them could not make a town, this experiment was an utter failure. The houses were never "habitable, but fell down before the finishing of them."

Equally futile was the attempt to turn the people from raising tobacco to the production of manufactured goods. After the expenditure of large sums on industrial plants, "for want of care the said houses were never finished . . . and the . . . manufactury wholly in a short time neglected and no good effected." Bacon's rebellious men denounced Berkeley's parasites "for having upon specious pretences of public works raised great unjust taxes upon the commonalty for the advancement of private favorites and other sinister ends, but no visible effects in any measure adequate."

Berkeley denied the charges of favoritism and misgovernment. He called on God to witness that he knew of nothing in which he had not distributed equal justice to all men. His friends rallied to his support. "The whole are sensible of his great integrity, constant care, and diligence," the Council wrote to the Lords of Trade. Bacon had loaded him with all the base calumnies and scandals, and with as much malice and ingratitude as all the black devils in hell could tempt him to. It was hard indeed that so good a governor should have his honor and reputation "ravished away" in his old age.

Though we may discount the testimony of those who had been partners with Berkeley in his misgovernment, it is clear that he was in no way responsible for the chief cause of poverty in the colony—the Navigation Acts. Prior to 1660 the Virginians carried on an extensive trade with Holland, selling their tobacco to Dutch merchants and taking Dutch manufactured goods in exchange. When the tobacco reached Holland it was "manufactured" and then distributed to other countries. This trade brought prosperity to the colony, for the Dutch paid well for the tobacco and sold their goods cheaply. But the Navigation Acts required that tobacco exported from the colonies must be shipped to England or to her dominions, and that manufactured goods imported must come from England.

The result was disastrous. England was not able by herself to consume the entire crop. Nor could the merchants re-export it to the continent because they did not have access to the markets. So the tobacco piled up in the English warehouses, while the price sank lower and lower. The Dutch had given three pence a pound for tobacco, but now the crop was sold at half a penny a pound. Formerly the poor planter who raised a thousand pounds of tobacco each year could count on an income of £12, which was ample for his needs. After the passage of the Navigation Acts he was fortunate if he made forty-five shillings. This was so little that Secretary Ludwell attributed it to nothing but the mercy of God that he had "not fallen into mutiny and confusion." In 1662 Berkeley and others complained that the price of tobacco was so low that it would not bear the charge of freight and customs, give encouragement to the merchants, and subsistence to the planters.

As though this were not enough, a series of disasters struck the colony bringing ruin and suffering in their wake. In 1667, when England and Holland were at war, a fleet of five Dutch warships entered Chesapeake Bay and captured the *Elizabeth*, an English frigate of forty-six guns. They then turned on the tobacco fleet and captured twenty vessels. Six years later nine Dutch warships came in and engaged the English in a desperate battle off Lynnhaven Bay while the tobacco ships scurried for shallow water. Unfortunately nine or ten ran aground and were taken.

Even nature seemed bent on completing the ruin of the planters. "This poor country . . . is now reduced to a very miserable condition by a continual course of misfortune," wrote Thomas Ludwell in 1667. "In April . . . we had a most prodigious storm of hail, many of them as big as turkey eggs, which destroyed most of our young mast and cattle. On the fifth of June following came the Dutch upon us. . . . They were not gone before it fell to raining and continued for forty days together. . . . But on the 27th of August followed the most dreadful hurricane that ever the colony groaned under. . . . The nearest computation is at least 10,000 houses blown down, all the Indian grain laid flat upon the ground, all the tobacco in the fields torn to pieces."

It was soon after the Restoration that the people of Virginia learned that "all the lands and water lying between Potomac and Rappahannock, together with all the royalties belonging thereto," had been granted to Lord Hopton and several other noblemen. In alarm they appealed "for relief" to the King, and were greatly relieved when the grant was recalled. And though another patent was issued, it contained reservations to protect "the rights, privileges, and properties of the inhabitants." But their joy was tempered by a provision giving the patentees the quit rents with eleven years arrears. This would be more than the entire value of many men's estates, it was complained.

So they employed agents to plead their cause in London. In the meanwhile the patent had been assigned to the Earl of St. Albans, Lord John Berkeley, Sir William Moreton, and John Trethney. When the agents proposed that they surrender their rights in return for a large sum of money to be raised by taxing the people of the colony, most of them agreed. But at this point the King issued a patent to the Earl of Arlington and Lord Culpeper, "which not only included the lands formerly granted . . . but all the rest of the colony." The Virginians were in despair. The two lords were to have many powers rightly belonging to the government. They were to pocket all escheats, quit rents, and duties belonging to the Crown; they had the power to create new counties and parishes, to issue patents for land; they could appoint sheriffs, surveyors, and other officers, and induct ministers. The Assembly complained that this nullified all previous charters and promises and made the people subjects to their fellow subjects.

So negotiations had to begin again. In the end Arlington and Culpeper agreed to give up their patent in return for a new one for the Northern Neck assuring them the quit rents and escheated property. Having gained this concession the agents then pleaded for a charter for the colony guaranteeing the liberties of the colonists. In it there were to be promises that they should continue to have their immediate dependence on the Crown, and that no tax should be laid upon them but by the consent of the Assembly. The King in Council assented to the charter, and twice it reached the Great Seal. But there it was held up. In the meanwhile news came of Bacon's Rebellion, and the King reversed his order. Later he did grant letters patent, but they contained little more than the promise that the colony should be directly dependent on the Crown.

This whole affair caused universal resentment in the colony, and the expense of the negotiations in England made the people "desperately uneasy." Berkeley reported that "the two great taxes of sixty pounds per poll to buy in the Northern patent made those that thought they were not concerned in it ripe for mutiny." The agents, too, warned that the Arlington and Culpeper grant might cause the common people to rise in arms and perhaps bring about "the utter dispersion" of the planters.

With the staple crop of the colony a drug on the market because of the Navigation Acts, with tax piled on tax to buy back the liberties of the people from favorites of the King, with self-government made a mockery by the corrupting of the Burgesses, with the small farmers in rags, the people were ready to rise in arms at the least excuse. Before young Nathaniel Bacon set foot on Virginia soil Berkeley and his henchmen were trembling in their boots. The governor thought that if an opportunity offered itself the planters might go over to the Dutch "in hopes of bettering their condition by sharing the plunder of the country with them."

Into this mass of dynamite an Indian war threw a torch. The resulting explosion was Bacon's Rebellion.

In 1674 two mutinies had failed, it was said because the

people, after assembling in arms, could not find a leader. Two years later, when again angry men gathered, they found their leader in Bacon. This young man was the son of Thomas Bacon, a wealthy English squire. At an early age he entered St. Catherine's Hall, Cambridge, as a fellow-commoner. There he seems to have idled away his time, and when he "broke into some extravagances" his father withdrew him. This apparent misfortune was turned to good effect when his father secured for him as tutor the great naturalist, John Ray. Ray found Nathaniel a lad of "very good parts and a quick wit," but "impatient of labor." When he was sixteen he accompanied Ray on a tour of Europe. On his return he re-entered Cambridge and later studied at Gray's Inn.

In 1670 he married Elizabeth, daughter of Sir Edward Duke. Her father had positively forbidden the match, and when she disobeyed him cut her off without one groat. But Thomas Bacon, and after Sir Edward's death, her brother John, made ample provision for the young couple. All would have been well had not Nathaniel been tricked by two sharpers in a deal with a guileless youth named Jason, and left with a long and tedious lawsuit.

It was at this juncture that he decided to seek his fortune in Virginia. There he might hope for quick advancement, because his cousin, also named Nathaniel Bacon, had attained a position of influence, and because he was related to Lady Berkeley, wife of the governor. Upon the advice of his grandmother, Lady Brooke, he left his wife behind until he had prepared a place for her "answerable to her quality." Upon his arrival in Virginia he was welcomed by Sir William, and it was at his advice "or at least friendly approbation" that he purchased a plantation at Curles Neck, on the James, forty miles above Jamestown, and a tract of land at the site of Richmond, on what was then the frontier. "When first I designed Virginia my chiefest aims were a further inquiry into those western parts in order to which I chose to seat myself so remote," he said, "I having always been delighted in solitude."

Bacon had been in Virginia but a few months when the governor appointed him to the Council of State. This seemed a great honor indeed for a young man of twenty-eight. But Berkeley explained: "Gentlemen of your quality come very rarely into this country, and therefore when they do come are used by me with all respect." Bacon was greatly surprised. "As to anything of public employment in the country, my tender age and manner of living, not free from follies and youthful excesses, forbad me to hope or expect any such thing. . . . This sudden change were enough to stagger a philosopher of more settled temper than I am."

But it was not possible for the dictatorial governor and the hotheaded youth to get along together. Berkeley was accustomed to having obedience in return for favors. Bacon was not the man to knuckle under. It was prophetic of what was to follow that the first difference grew out of relations with the allied Indians. When poor immigrants took up holdings on the frontier rather than become tenants to wealthy men in the east, they encroached on the reservations of those Indian tribes which were under the protection of the government. They even laid out farms within the very limits of their villages. When the Indians, driven by hunger, killed any of their cattle or hogs, the frontiersmen "beat and abused them."

Apparently it was a dispute with the Indians which caused the first temporary breach between Bacon and Berkeley. We do not know just what happened, but Bacon in a letter to the Governor speaks of his "unbecoming deportment in your Honor's presence," and said he was sorry for it. Sir William's reply makes it probable that Bacon had suffered some losses from neighboring Indians, and had retaliated. "This sudden business of the Indians," Berkeley said, had raised in him "high distemper." And he asked Bacon to consider that relations between the whites and the Indians was his responsibility, so that it was important that he be advised of all dealings with them. Should there be serious trouble he would be criticised both in England and Virginia.

Bacon must have resented Berkeley's monopoly of the fur trade. He tells us that a desire to have a share in this lucrative business had been one of his motives for settling on the frontier. But he made a virtue of necessity and, in partnership with his neighbor, William Byrd I, applied to the governor for a license. They would pay him 800 pounds of beaver fur for the first year and 600 pounds a year thereafter. This looked good to Sir William. "I am in no such plentiful condition that I should refuse a good offer," he replied, "and therefore am likely to accept your and my cousin Byrd's offer."

With the opening months of 1676 there were ominous rumblings of revolt. From New England came word that the English there were engaged in a deadly war with the Indians, which Berkeley thought was not merely a local affair, "but a general combination of all from New England thither." The so-called allied tribes on the Virginia frontiers were sullen and resentful. "They also would be rid of us if they could," said Berkeley. Their efforts to wipe out the English in previous wars had failed only because their bows and arrows were no match for the muskets of the English. Now that they had firearms might not their efforts be more successful?

It was the Marylanders who had given firearms to the Susquehannocks, a fierce tribe living on their northern border. This they did so that they could protect them from the Senecas, one of the tribes of the Iroquois confederation. But in 1674, when the Marylanders made a separate treaty with the Senecas, the latter fell on the Susquehannocks, defeated them in battle, and swept them out of their fortified villages. Fleeing through Maryland the remnant of the tribe established themselves on the north bank of the Potomac directly across from the site of Mount Vernon.

Here they were safe from their enemies, but not from hunger. They might catch fish from the river, but they lacked space for corn fields, and the plantations of the English spread out over what had once been hunting grounds. It was inevitable that they would seek food where they could find it, and having robbed nearby farms they could not resist the temptation to commit a few murders. Associated with them were the remnants of the Doegs who had been driven out of Virginia a few years before because of the "execrable murders" they had committed.

In the summer of 1675 a party of Indians paddled across the Potomac, and after killing several men, made good their escape back to Maryland. Shortly afterwards people returning from church found a man covered with ghastly wounds lying across his threshold, who managed to gasp out, "Doegs, Doegs." Immediately the alarm was sounded, and a party of thirty or more men assembled on the south bank of the river opposite the Indian reservation under the command of Colonel George Mason and Captain George Brent.

At dawn they crossed over to the Maryland side. Here they divided their forces, Mason leading part in one direction through the woods and Brent the other in another. Brent came upon a cabin full of Doegs. Their chief denied knowledge of the murders, but when he started to run Brent shot him. At this the Indians in the cabin made a dash for safety in the face of a volley which brought down ten of them.

In the meanwhile Mason, too, had come upon a cabin full of Indians, and had killed fourteen of them. But when he found out that they were not Doegs but Susquehannocks, he shouted: "For the Lord's sake shoot no more, these are our friends the Susquehannocks." But they now were their friends no longer. They began a series of bloody raids in Stafford County on the

Courtesy Cook Collection, Valentine Museum. From Frank Leslie's Illustrated Newspaper, Sept. 6, 1866

Bacon's Castle, Surry County, Virginia

STRANGE NEWS
FROM
VIRGINIA;
Being a full and true
ACCOUNT
OF THE
LIFE and DEATH
OF
Nathanael Bacon Esquire,

Who was the only Cause and Original of all the late Troubles in that COUNTRY.

With a full Relation of all the Accidents which have happened in the late War there between the Christians and Indians.

LONDON,
Printed for *William Harris*, next door to the Turn-Stile without *Moor-gate*. 1677.

From the Church Catalogue
Photo by T. L. Williams

Virginia side of the river and Charles County in Maryland. Governor Calvert was quite right in complaining to Berkeley of the invasion of his province by an armed force to turn friendly Indians into mortal enemies.

But since it was now too late to restore peace, the Virginians and Marylanders agreed upon a joint campaign to force the Susquehannocks to leave the region and give hostages for their peaceful conduct. It was late in September when the Maryland troops, under Major Thomas Trueman, arrived on the north bank of the Piscataway Creek, the site of Fort Washington. A few days later a body of Virginians under Colonel John Washington, great-grandfather of George Washington, and Colonel Isaac Allerton, landed from a fleet of sloops.

Across the creek, on a low bit of land, protected by patches of swamp, the Susquehannocks had built a fort. Had it been no more than a round stockade, after the traditional Indian style, it could have been taken with ease. But the Marylanders themselves had taught the Susquehannocks the art of fortification. So they had laid out a large square, raised embankments on all four sides, with an outer defence of palisades, and a ditch between. At each corner was a bastion, from which an attacking force could be enfiladed. Lacking artillery to batter down these works the three commanders decided to invest the fort and starve out the defenders.

In the meanwhile Major Trueman invited the "great men" to a parley. When five of them came out, he charged them with recent murders in Maryland. The Indians placed the blame on prowling bands of Senecas. This was an obvious lie, for Susquehannocks had been seen wearing the clothing of some of the murdered whites, and raiding parties had come directly to the fort, their canoes laden with beef. Seeing himself in imminent danger, one of the Indians produced a medal bearing the image of Lord Baltimore, and a paper which he said was a pledge from a former governor of Maryland to protect the tribe from harm.

Despite this, and despite the fact that the "great men" had come under a truce to discuss peace, Trueman ordered his men to knock them on the head.

When word of this outrage reached Governor Berkeley he was furious. "If they had killed my grandfather and my grandmother, my father and mother and all my friends, yet if they had come to treat of peace, they ought to have gone in peace," he blurted out. Major Trueman was impeached in Maryland, fined and sentenced to imprisonment, but this did not undo the wrong or prevent the terrible consequences.

The Indians in the fort put up a desperate resistance. Weeks passed, and they still held out. To every suggestion of parley they asked: "Where are our great men?" At last, when "brought to great distress" through hunger, they broke through the encircling English with their wives and children, and vanished into the forest. Making their way up the Maryland side of the river, they crossed over to Virginia, and began a series of raids upon the frontier plantations on the upper Rappahannock and Mattapony rivers.

Within a few days they had killed sixty persons. The fortunate ones were those who fell at the first volley, for the miserable captives were subjected to tortures that would have baffled the imagination of a Dante. "Some they roast alive, offering their flesh to such English prisoners as they keep languishing by a lingering death, pulling their nails off, making holes and sticking feathers in their flesh. Some they rip open and make run their guts round trees."

For the moment the old spirit which had made him so ardent a fighter in the English Civil War and in the battles against Opechancanough flared anew in Governor Berkeley. Calling together a force of horse and foot, he placed them under the command of Sir Henry Chicheley with orders to pursue the murderers. But when all was ready and Chicheley was expecting the order to march Berkeley changed his mind, withdrew his commission and disbanded his forces.

This sudden change has long puzzled historians. Berkeley himself had taken the lead in carrying the war to the enemy following the massacre of 1644; why did he hang back now? It may have been the offer of peace from the new chief of the Susquehannocks, which Sir William was willing to accept but which the Indians themselves ignored. It may have been the fear that Chicheley's men might not discriminate between friend and foe and by attacking some of the allied Indians involve them in the war. He stated later that he would have preserved those Indians so that they could be his "spies and intelligence to find out the more bloody enemies." Certainly in this he was foreshadowing the policy followed by his successors for more than a century. But it did not justify leaving the frontier open to attack, while the murders and torturing continued.

It is not necessary to accept the accusation of Bacon and his followers that Berkeley adopted this policy so as not to interfere with the beaver trade. It might have been effective had not the Pamunkeys, the Appomatox, and other nearby tribes been dissatisfied and resentful. As it was, the governor was soon obliged to abandon it. "As soon as I had the least intelligence that they were our treacherous enemies I have given out commissions to destroy them all," he said. To Colonel Goodrich, when he was about to lead an expedition up the Rappahannock, he wrote: "I believe all the Indians, our neighbors, are engaged with the Susquehannocks, therefore I desire you to spare none . . . for they are all our enemies."

Berkeley blamed Bacon and his men for the defection of the allied Indians. It was they, he said, who had driven them out of their towns and forced them "to live remote in the woods." It was only then, when they became desperate through hunger, that they joined in the raids on the English. One can never be certain which side started hostilities. Probably both were to blame. But Berkeley did not stop to consider that the fault was basically his own. Had he not granted all the best lands in the east to his favorites, poor planters would not have had to encroach on the Indian reservations, in which case the Indians might have remained peaceful, and even fought side by side with the English against the Susquehannocks.

After recalling the expedition under Chicheley, Berkeley remained inactive until, in February, he received word that the Indians had made new raids. Then he summoned the Assembly. Several weeks passed before they convened, since it took time to reach the Burgesses who lived in the distant counties, and for them to travel, perhaps by boat, down the Potomac or the Rappahannock, and up the James to Jamestown. At last, on March 7, the session opened.

Berkeley had determined on a defensive war, and the Assembly obediently carried out his wishes. So they declared war on all Indians who were known to have taken part in the murderous raids, provided for the enlistment of friendly Indians, called out a force of 500 men, prohibited trade in firearms with the savages, and ordered the erection of eight forts on the frontiers.

This policy might have been successful had Berkeley made the forts bases for expeditions against the enemy. The Indians seem to have made their raids in small parties, and with rangers spying upon them, forces could have rushed out from the nearest fort to intercept or pursue them. In fact this seems to have been Berkeley's original plan. The spread of hostilities "puts us on an absolute necessity not only of fortifying our frontiers more strongly, but of keeping several considerable parties of both horse and foot still in motion to confront them wherever they shall attack us," he wrote in a report to the English government late in March.

Berkeley stated that the forts served their purpose well. "In April and May we lost not one man," he stated. But this Bacon and his men denied. Even when a garrison received word that Indians were near, they were not permitted to pursue them until they had notified the governor, who might be fifty or sixty miles away, and received his permission. The forts proved useless, they said, for the Indians sneaked in between them and fell upon the outlying plantations, burning, plundering, and killing. This it was easy to do in a country full of "thick woods, swamps, and other covert." So, as houses went up in flames, as men, women, and children were murdered, as miserable captives were led off to await torture, a cry arose for relief. What is needed, people said, is some considerable force in motion to seek out the enemy and destroy them.

So petition after petition came to Berkeley begging him to send them a leader. We have the arms, they said, all we ask is permission to defend ourselves. But they met with peremptory refusal. As one group stood before him, hat in hand, one of them spoke of themselves as his honor's subjects. "Why you are a set of fools and loggerheads. You are the King's subjects, and so am I," Berkeley blurted out. "A pox take you."

The frontier planters were in despair. Many deserted their homes and fled to the more settled parts of the country. Some declared they would plant no more tobacco, since it would be taken from them to pay for the useless forts. And they were deeply angered when it was reported to them that Berkeley had said that if they had no tobacco, "they had cows and feather beds sufficient to discharge their levies." At last, "the cries of their women and children growing grievous and intolerable to them," and hearing that large bodies of Indians were encamped on the upper James ready to descend on them, the people of Charles City County assembled in arms near Merchants Hope.

They found their leader in Nathaniel Bacon. Bacon, despite his youth, was looked up to as one of the Council, and a member of the English gentry. Not only did he sympathize with the people in their fear and hatred of the Indians, but he had a personal grievance, since they had plundered his outer plantation and killed his overseer. So when several of his neighbors urged him to cross the James to visit the men in arms, he readily consented.

When they saw the slender, black-haired youth, they set up a great cry: "A Bacon! A Bacon! A Bacon!" This was too much for him to resist. It is stated by one of the old chroniclers that he had "a most imperious and dangerous hidden pride of heart." The leadership thus thrust upon him must have pleased him. He was now no longer the erratic youth who had been withdrawn from Cambridge, had caused his father great trouble and anxiety, and had been duped by sharpers. He was the leader of men. But there can be no doubt that he yielded to the pleas of his friends and neighbors in part at least because of his loathing of the Indians and his horror at their cruelty. He yielded also because his spirit revolted at Berkeley's system of government by corruption, because he sympathized with the people in their outcry against the killing burdens placed on them, and because he hoped to redress their grievances. His rough followers listened with approval as he denounced the government as "negligent and wicked, treacherous and incapable, the laws unjust and oppressive," and declared that reform was absolutely necessary. So he listed their names on a huge round-robin, and "enjoined them by an oath to stick fast together and to him." As word spread throughout the colony that at last the people had a champion, almost overnight he became the popular hero, and "the only patron of the country and the preserver of their lives and fortunes."

He first wrote Berkeley asking for a commission to go out to attack the Indians, and then, without waiting for a reply, crossed the Chickahominy into New Kent to overawe or perhaps attack the Pamunkeys. He found the people of this county "ripe for rebellion" and eager to wipe out their treacherous neighbors. But when he heard that the Pamunkeys had fled from their villages to the inaccessible Dragon's Swamp, he turned back to pursue a body of Susquehannocks who had moved south to the Roanoke river.

When the news reached Berkeley that the frontier planters had assembled in arms, chosen Bacon their leader, denounced his administration, and driven the Pamunkeys into hiding, he was furious. But as he had broken up previous mutinies by proclamations, he tried the same expedient now. He declared the action of Bacon and his men illegal and rebellious. But pardon would be granted provided they disperse at once and return to their duty and allegiance.

Bacon had already written the governor to assure him that in taking up arms he was acting only in self-defense and for the country's safety. But now he sent another letter reiterating that he had no evil intentions to him or the government. "I am now going out to seek a more agreeable destiny than you are pleased to design me," he added. As to the money he owed him he enclosed an order for its payment.

He then turned his back on the settlements and plunged into the forests. Although he said he distrusted all Indians, he went out of his way to enlist a few warriors from the allied Nottoways and Meherrins. He then followed a trail used by fur traders and headed for an island in the Roanoke river. Here a friendly tribe, the Occaneechees, had established two forts and a village. They welcomed Bacon, ferried his men over to the island, and went themselves to attack a band of Susquehannocks in a nearby fort. With the aid of some Mannikins, whom the Susquehannocks had forced to accompany them, they took the fort and came back leading a number of captives.

Having accomplished what he had set out to do without the loss of a man, Bacon probably would have started home, had he had provisions enough for the long march through the wilderness. As it was his men faced starvation. So he demanded supplies of food from the Occaneechee chief. Berkeley's friends later accused him of demanding also beaver taken from the Susquehannock fort. The ensuing dispute led to a bloody battle on the island, in which the English rushed up to the palisaded fort, began firing in at the portholes, and set fire to the village. The next day the Indians sallied out, and hiding behind trees, tried to pick off the English. But when many of their warriors had been killed, the chief, with twenty men, tried to circle the English. This too failed, the chief was killed, and the remaining Indians with their wives and children, taking to their canoes, made their escape. Bacon and his men gathered up the spoils, plundered the Occaneechee larder, swam their horses over to the mainland, and started on the return march.

When Berkeley found that his proclamation had had no effect, he gathered a force of about three hundred men, and set out for the falls of the James. But he was too late. When he arrived Bacon and his men had disappeared into the forest on their way to the Roanoke. So the governor had to content himself with issuing another proclamation. Nathaniel Bacon, junior, of Henrico County, with divers rude, dissolute, and tumultuous persons, contrary to the laws of England and their allegiance to the King, had taken up arms without obtaining from him any order or commission. Since this tended to the ruin and overthrow of the government, he declared that Bacon and his aiders were unlawful, mutinous, and rebellious.

At the same time, Lady Berkeley issued a statement of her own. It had been rumored among the people that Bacon would not only be their captain, but provide out of his own pocket for their wives and children. This was a vain hope, she said. His entire estate was bound over, his father had refused to honor his bills of exchange, he owed William Byrd £400 and his cousin Colonel Nathaniel Bacon, senior, £200. "I do accuse him of a worse crime than poverty," she added, "I do accuse him of ingratitude, and that of a deep dye, to return the favorable amity of the governor with casting all kinds of aspersions upon his courage and conduct in the government of this colony."

In the meanwhile, awaiting Bacon's return, the governor turned his attention to the defences on the upper James. He commanded the queen of the Pamunkeys to return to her reservation, and when she refused, prepared to drive her out of the Dragon Swamp. But at this moment word reached him that the people in all parts of the colony were rising against him. Now that they had a leader to redress their wrongs, in many an humble cabin men seized their fusils, swords, and halberds, and waited for him to call them to his side. They expected him to end corruption and favoritism in the government, to lower taxes, to correct private injustices, to give them a really representative Assembly.

Berkeley was astonished. Hastening back to Green Spring he questioned his Council. What do they want? What have I done in all the years I have been governor to turn so many thousands against me? What do you advise me to do? The Council replied that his keeping the Assembly for so many years was one of the chief grievances and advised him to have a new election. Later he stated that it was Bacon who made "the rabble cry out for a new Assembly." Reluctantly he complied. He had every reason to expect that the new House of Burgesses would be overwhelmingly hostile to him, and as the returns came in he saw that his worst fears would be realized. The final count showed that one after another the old Burgesses were defeated at the polls until in the end all but eight of the new House were of "Bacon's faction."

When Bacon returned from the Occaneechee fight, he was elated with the acclaim of the people, not only on the frontier but in all parts of the colony, but he was aggrieved that the governor had proclaimed him a rebel and threatened his life. On May 25, he wrote to Berkeley: "I am sorry to find that for the expence of our estates and hazard of our lives in the country's service we should by misinformers have our true intentions so falsely represented to you. . . . We have all along manifested our abhorrence of mutiny and rebellion. . . . If your honor were in person to lead or command I would follow and obey." But then he continued with a veiled threat. If he sought to revenge himself he had only to listen to all the stories of "your honor's falsehood, cowardice, treachery, receiving bribes." He had heard that Lady Berkeley had raised "several scandalous and false reports" against him, that he was not worth a groat and that his notes had been protested. He could hear enough about her, he retorted, if he would permit himself to listen.

When Berkeley showed this letter to the Council, they wrote Bacon: "Our advice to you is that the most honorable, the most secure, and most safe way for yourself [is for] you forthwith in the most humble manner present yourself to the governor and, acknowledging your errors, humbly crave his pardon." If he preferred to justify his conduct, they promised him a fair trial either in Virginia or in England.

But with the plaudits of the people ringing in his ears, Bacon was unwilling to humble himself. "My submissions are unacceptable, my real intentions misunderstood," he wrote Berkeley. "I am sorry that your honor's resentments are of such violence and growth as to command my appearance with all contempt and disgrace and my disowning and belying so glorious a cause as the country's defence. I know my person safe in your honor's word, but only beg what pledge or warranty I shall have for my reputation."

So, when the sheriff of Henrico rose in court to read Berkeley's proclamation, he was interrupted by Bacon, who was there with thirty or forty of his men. "If you dare read a line of that proclamation, I will make you regret it," he said. Then, as though to show their defiance of the governor, the people elected Bacon and his ardent friend, Captain James Crews, to represent them in the House of Burgesses.

It would have been well for Bacon had he chosen to ride down to Jamestown with a heavy escort. Instead he decided on the easier and usual method of travel by boat, and so set out in his sloop with forty armed men. On June 6, when they came abreast Jamestown, they were fired on by the guns of the fort. So they turned about and sailed further up the river. With the coming of darkness Bacon, with twenty of his men, rowed ashore, and held a long conference with Richard Lawrence and William Drummond, Berkeley's inveterate enemies. It is obvious that Bacon had known these men before. It is even possible that he had boarded at Mrs. Lawrence's tavern while a member of the Council, and that her husband had done his best to turn him against Sir William with charges of arbitrary and corrupt government.

One wishes that one might have sat in on that night meeting. What did the young popular leader discuss with these two embittered men? The Indian war beyond doubt. But also Berkeley's "French despotism," and how best to curb it. With an Assembly hostile to Berkeley in session, Lawrence and Drummond must have recognized their chance. In fact Berkeley had warned the Burgesses not to be misled by these "two rogues." So it seems extremely probable that they drilled Bacon on what measures to propose when he took his seat in the House.

At early dawn, when Bacon was returning, he was discovered and chased up the river by several armed boats. He seems to have reached his sloop, but when he tried to escape up the river, he was forced under the guns of the *Adam and Eve*, a warship commanded by Captain Thomas Gardiner, and forced to surrender.

When Bacon was led before the governor, the old man exclaimed: "Now I behold the greatest rebel that ever was in Virginia."

Then, after a pause, he asked: "Mr. Bacon, have you forgot to be a gentleman?"

"No, may it please your honor."

"Then, I'll take your parole."

Soon after this scene Bacon had a conference with his cousin in which the latter pleaded with him to make his submission and give up the idea of reforming the government and going out to fight the Indians. If he would promise to do so, he said, he would turn over to him a part of his estate and leave him the remainder after his own and his wife's deaths. In the end the younger Bacon yielded and signed a paper engaging to refrain from further disobedience to the government.

A few days later the governor summoned the Burgesses to meet with the Council in the Court Room of the State House. When all were seated he stood up and said: "If there be joy in the presence of the angels over one sinner that repenteth, there is joy now, for we have a penitent sinner come before us. Call Mr. Bacon."

When Bacon stepped forward, fell on his knees, and handed in his submission, the governor resumed: "God forgive you! I forgive you!"

"And all that were with him?" asked one of the Councillors.

"Yes, and all that were with him," replied the governor.

"Mr. Bacon,'" he added, "if you will live civilly but till next Quarter Court, I will promise to restore you again to your place there." But he decided not to wait so long, and the following day permitted him to resume his seat.

We are left in no doubt as to why Berkeley was so lenient. "Why did I not put him to death when I had him in my power?" he asked later. "I must have been judge, jury, and executioner to have done it, for the Assembly . . . were all picked for him. The Council frightened with hearing 2000 men were armed to deliver him." Philip Ludwell wrote Lady Berkeley who a few weeks before had sailed for England, that she must wonder why instead of death "such favors were heaped on." But it was unavoidable, since hundreds of enraged men were within a day's march of Jamestown, and the forces at hand to oppose them secretly in sympathy with Bacon. "There is not a part of the country free from the infection. Never was there so great a madness as the people generally were seized with."

But in restoring Bacon to the Council Berkeley was no doubt

actuated as much by policy as by fear, for it was better to have him there where he could keep his eye on him than in the House of Burgesses where he might attempt to carry through reform legislation.

By this time anyone less stubborn and arbitrary than Berkeley would have learned his lesson. On June 12, when Bacon was still in the governor's power, Philip Ludwell wrote his brother: "It now looks like general ruin for the country. . . . The governor seems determined to leave for England. . . . If he does he leaves a lost country." Had he given Bacon a commission to fight the Indians and permitted the Assembly to carry out adequate reforms in the government, the people might have been satisfied. But when the Assembly met things seemed to be going in the old way.

If we are to understand the transactions of this historic Assembly it is necessary to divide the session into two parts, the part when Berkeley had Bacon in his power, and the part when Bacon had escaped and was once more at the head of his army. During the first part Berkeley seems to have dominated the Assembly despite the pro-Bacon majority, during the second part the threat of coercion by Bacon's angry frontiersmen undoubtedly affected all legislation. Without this division many of the known facts seem incongruous and conflicting; with it they fit together like the pieces of a jig-saw puzzle.

At the opening of the session "some gentlemen took this opportunity to endeavor the redressing several grievances the country then labored under," and a committee was about to be named for this purpose when they "were interrupted by pressing messages from the governor to meddle with nothing until the Indian business was dispatched." So the matter of grievances was sidetracked.

Then followed a heated debate on whether the House would ask that two Councillors sit with the committee on Indian Affairs. In the end "this was huddled off without coming to a vote, and so the committee must submit to be overawed, and have every carped at expression carried straight to the governor."

And the governor, closing his eyes to the fact that the Pamunkeys hated the English and were sullen and resentful, insisted that they return to their towns and join in the defence of the colony. So their queen was brought in and asked how many men she would furnish. In reply she reproached the English for not giving her people compensation for their aid in a former war in which her husband had been killed. In the end she promised twelve men, but it must have been obvious to all that she and they were not to be trusted. When she had gone the committee proceeded with their plans for prosecuting the war. Some of the forts were to be abandoned and their garrisons distributed among fourteen frontier plantations, and an army of 1,000 men was to be raised and sent out against the enemy.

Bacon was a discontented spectator of these proceedings. The governor was as overbearing as ever, the Burgesses were overawed, the plans for reform were set aside, the Indian war was mismanaged. He must have been disgusted that the Burgesses were too cowardly to vote down a resolution requesting the governor not to resign. The Assembly did not prove "answerable to our expectations", he said later, for which he thought they should be censured. So, telling Berkeley that his wife was ill, he got permission to visit her. No sooner had he gone than the governor heard that he intended to place himself once more at the head of his volunteer army. In desperate haste horsemen galloped off to intercept him. But they were too late. Bacon had made good his escape.

In Henrico angry men gathered around him. And when he told them that the governor had not given him a commission and that he still persisted in carrying out essentially the old plan for the war, they were furious. In Bacon's absence the Indians had renewed their raids, and had wiped out many whole families.

The frontiersmen vowed that they would have a commission or they would march on Jamestown and "pull down the town."

So off they went, some mounted, others on foot. There was talk of sharing the estates of the rich, of making Lady Berkeley discard her fine gowns for "canvas linen," of ending all taxes. "Thus the raging torrent came down to town."

When the governor heard that they were coming he made desperate efforts to gather a force to resist them. But it was too late. It was rumored that Bacon had threatened that if a gun was fired at his men he would "kill and destroy all." Since resistance was useless, Berkeley threw the guns from their carriages and waited for Bacon's arrival.

So the motley band came streaming into town. "Now tag, rag and bobtail carry a high hand." Bacon drew up a double line before the State House and demanded that some members of the Council come out to confer with him. When Colonel Spencer and Colonel Cole appeared he told them he had come for a commission. Then he said that the people would not submit to taxes to pay for the proposed new army. And his men shouted: "No levies! No levies!"

At this juncture Berkeley rushed out, gesticulating wildly and denouncing Bacon to his face as a traitor.

Then he threw back his coat and shouted: "Here, shoot me, 'fore God, fair mark, shoot."

Bacon replied that he would not hurt a hair of his head. They had come for a commission to save their lives from the Indians, which had so often been promised.

The Burgesses hearing the noise below, crowded to the windows. But they drew back when the soldiers pointed their fusils at them, calling out: "We will have it. We will have it." One of the Burgesses called back: "For God's sake hold your hands; forbear a little and you shall have what you please."

After walking up and down before the State House for some

time, muttering threats and "new coined oaths," Bacon mounted the steps to the Long Room, where the Burgesses sat, and demanded a commission to lead a force out against the Indians. One of them told him that governor alone had the right to grant a commission. But when he left they sent a message to Sir William advising him to issue the commission. The Council, too, pointing out that he and they were in Bacon's power, added their voices. At last, though with intense bitterness, he yielded.

But new humiliations awaited him. He was forced to write the King justifying Bacon's conduct, sign blank commissions for Bacon's officers, and imprison some of his most loyal friends. So long as it did not concern "life and limb" he was willing to do anything to be rid of him.

In his determination to secure a commission Bacon did not neglect the matter of reform. When Berkeley suggested that they decide their controversy by a duel with swords, he replied that "he came for redress of the people's grievances." In the Assembly he "pressed hard, nigh an hour's harangue on preserving our lives from the Indians, inspecting the revenues, the exorbitant taxes, and redressing the grievances and calamities of that deplorable country." After this impassioned plea he must have been greatly surprised when the Assembly told him "that they had already redressed their grievances." Since, had the so-called Bacon's Laws been passed while he was sitting in the Council he would have known it, they must have been rushed through during the brief period between his flight from Jamestown and his return.

It will be helpful to recall the situation in the little capital at the time. With hundreds of enraged frontiersmen "within a day's journey", with no force which could be trusted to oppose them, the governor and his friends were in a state of panic. Even before Bacon's escape Ludwell wrote: "We have all the reason in the world to suspect their designs are ruinous." And now, with Bacon back at their head to tell them of his humiliation and report that he still had no commission, Berkeley feared the worst. Then came the certain information that Bacon was marching on the town.

Obviously the Assembly and the governor rushed Bacon's Laws through in a desperate, last minute attempt to appease Bacon and his men. When the governor affixed his signature he must have been almost within hearing distance of the tramp of armed men. And it is significant that both the governor and the Assembly wished to have the laws read before Bacon's men "for their satisfaction." That Bacon, who was in no humor to be appeased, refused to permit this, is no indication that he did not heartily approve of the laws.

We do not know who drew up Bacon's Laws. It may have been Lawrence and Drummond, who introduced them through some ally in the House. It may have been Bacon's neighbor, Thomas Blayton, whom Colonel Edward Hill afterwards called "Bacon's great engine" in the Assembly. It may have been James Minge, clerk of the Assembly, "another [of] Bacon's great friends in forming the laws." More probably it was the committee on grievances. But whoever drew them up, whoever introduced them, most of the credit goes to Bacon. They were aimed at the abuses he repeatedly denounced, they were passed in an Assembly which Bacon had incited the people to demand and which Berkeley declared overwhelmingly pro-Bacon, and signed under the threat of Bacon's armed forces.

Although the governor and the King both voided Bacon's Laws and the Assembly of February 1677 repealed them, they constitute a landmark in the development of self-government in Virginia. They broadened the franchise by giving the right to vote to all freemen; they gave the voters representation in the county courts in assessing taxes; they put an end to self-perpetuating vestries; they fixed the fees of sheriffs, collectors, and other officials; they made it illegal for sheriffs to serve more than one year at a time; no person could hold two of the offices of sheriff, clerk of the court, surveyor, or escheator at the same time; members of the Council were barred from sitting on the county courts.

It was long recognized in both England and America that liberty is grounded on the principle that no man's money can be taken from him without his own consent. Yet local taxes in Virginia, which often exceeded those voted by the Assembly, were assessed by the county courts made up of the governor's appointees. The self-perpetuating vestries also had the right to tax, for they levied the parish charges. Thus Bacon's Laws struck at an exceedingly dangerous abuse. The use of fees to raise money without the consent of the voters was a source of bitter controversy between the governors and the people for many decades to come, a controversy which culminated in the celebrated case of the pistole fee which got Governor Dinwiddie into so much trouble. The restricting of local officers to one office at a time struck a blow at Berkeley's system of government by placemen. But the laws did not include an act to prohibit officeholders from sitting in the Assembly. This would have gone to the root of the trouble, but it was too much to expect the governor to assent to it even with Bacon and his infuriated men marching on Jamestown. In fact, this step was taken only more than half a century later.

Bacon now began preparations for the Indian campaign. Riding from one county to another he gathered armed bands, appointed their officers, and sent them off to the falls of the James. Arms, ammunition, and stores were sent up the rivers in sloops. The well-to-do planters were angered when their horses and corn were taken for the expedition, but at any show of resistance they were threatened and intimidated. One of Bacon's men told John Mann, "with many fearful oaths, as God damn his blood, sink him and rot him, he would ruin him."

It was late in July when Bacon drew up his army of seven hundred horse and six hundred foot. Riding out before them, he made a brief address. He assured them of his loyalty to the King, and that it was "the cries of his brethren's blood" that induced him to secure his commission. He then took the oath of allegiance, and required the men to swear fidelity to him as their general. Then they broke ranks for the night, expecting the next day to march.

At that moment word arrived that Berkeley was busy raising forces with which to attack them in the rear. This forced Bacon to change all his plans. After the rebels had left for the frontier, the Governor, realizing that the sentiment of the colony was overwhelmingly against him, at first had made no attempt to resist him. But Philip Ludwell and Robert Beverley drew up a petition in the name of the people of Gloucester, stating that Bacon had stripped them of arms and asking the governor to protect them. Although "not five persons knew about it," Berkeley accepted it as a call to action. "This petition is most willingly granted," he wrote. It was his duty to protect the King's loyal subjects. Bacon's commission was illegal, he added, since it had been extracted by force.

In a spirit of elation he rode over to Gloucester and sent out a call for the militia to assemble. But when they learned that they were expected to fight against Bacon, the popular hero, they demurred. "For Bacon at that time was so much the hope and darling of the people that the governor's interest proved but weak and his friends so very few that he grew sick of the essay." As he rode out before the troops he heard a murmur, "Bacon! Bacon! Bacon!" and saw them walk away. Bitterly disappointed and wearied by his exertions, he fainted away in the saddle.

Upon receiving the news that the governor was trying to raise forces to oppose him, Bacon "causes the drums to beat and trumpets to sound for calling his men together." Then he addressed them. It was revenge which hurried the governor and his advisors on without regard to the people's safety. They would rather see them murdered and their ghosts sent to join those of their slaughtered friends, than have them disturb their trade with the Indians. So now they must use their swords in their own defence. While they were sound at heart and not wearied they must descend to find out why these men sought to destroy their lives who sought to preserve theirs.

At this there was a shout of "Amen! Amen!" They were all ready and would rather die on the field of battle than be hanged like rogues or perish in the woods at the hands of the merciless savages. So with muttered oaths they turned their faces toward Gloucester.

Hearing that Bacon's enraged men were pouring down upon them, Berkeley and his friends were at a loss as to what to do. If they fell into his hands imprisonment was the mildest treatment they could expect. It was Robert Beverley who suggested that they flee to Accomac, where they would be safe beyond the waters of the Chesapeake Bay. Berkeley agreed, and asked Sir Henry Chicheley to accompany him. Chicheley promised to join him later, but before he could get away was captured. Berkeley, Beverley, and three others procured a small vessel, and reached the Eastern Shore in safety. And for the next few days the bay was dotted with sails as one gentleman after another fled with his wife and children, leaving his house, furniture, crops, horses, and cattle to be plundered by Bacon's men.

This was the situation when Bacon returned from the frontier. With Berkeley in exile, and with the Council dispersed, the colony had been left without a government. So Bacon had to become dictator, assume the role of a Cromwell. He might well have become hopelessly confused had he not had Lawrence and Drummond to advise him in every step in taking over the government. Probably it was they who helped him draw up a manifesto, in which he dwelt on Berkeley's tyranny and injustice. All men were witnesses of the corruption of the government, it stated; how men of lowly estate, elevated to important posts, had lined their pockets at the public expense. If he had attacked the so-called allied Indians, it was because they had committed "murder upon murder" upon the settlers. Had the governor himself not supplied them with arms and ammunition the frontier plantations would not now be deserted, the blood of their brothers spilled.

Bacon set up headquarters at Middle Plantation, the site of Williamsburg. Here he issued a proclamation declaring Berkeley, Chicheley, Ludwell, Beverley, and others, traitors, and threatened to confiscate their estates unless they surrendered within four days. Next he summoned all the leading planters to a conference. When seventy had assembled, most of them because they feared to stay away, some because they were dragged in by force, Bacon asked them to take three oaths; that they would join with him against the Indians; that they would arrest anyone trying to raise troops against him; and lastly, to oppose any English troops sent to Virginia until Bacon could plead his case before the King. Many of those present demurred at the last oath, but in the end no less than sixty-nine signed, among them such prominent men as Thomas Swan, John Page, Philip Lightfoot, and Thomas Ballard.

It was shortly after this that Bacon had a conversation with a certain John Goode, of Henrico, which is revealing of his fears, hopes, and plans for the future.

"There is a report that Sir William Berkeley hath sent to the King for 2000 redcoats, and I do believe it may be true," said Bacon. "Tell me your opinion, may not 500 Virginians beat them, we having the same advantages against them the Indians have against us?"

"I rather conceive 500 redcoats may either subject or ruin Virginia," Goode replied.

"You talk strangely. Are not we acquainted with the country, can lay ambushes, and take to trees and put them by the use of their discipline, and are doubtless as good or better shots than they."

"But they can accomplish what I have said without hazard . . . by taking opportunities of landing where there shall be no opposition, firing our houses and fences, destroying our stock and preventing all trade. . . ."

"There may be such prevention that they shall not be able to make any great progress in such mischiefs. And the country and clime not agreeing with their constitutions, great mortality will happen amongst them. . . ."

"You see, sir, . . . all the principal men in the country dislike your manner of proceedings. They, you may be sure, will join with the redcoats."

To this Bacon replied that he would see to it that they did not.

"Sir, you speak as though you designed a total defection from his Majesty and our country."

"Why, have not many princes lost their dominions so?" he asked, smiling.

"They have been people as have been able to subsist without their princes. The poverty of Virginia is such that the major part of the inhabitants can scarce supply their wants from hand to mouth, and many there are besides who can hardly shift without supply one year, and you may be sure that the people which so fondly follow you, when they come to feel the miserable wants of food and raiment, will be in greater haste to leave you than they were to come after you. Besides, here are many people in Virginia that receive considerable benefits . . . in England, and many which expect patrimonies. . . ."

"For supply I know nothing the country will not be able to provide for itself withal in a little time save ammunition and iron, and I believe the King of France or States of Holland would either of them entertain a trade with us."

"Sir, our King is a great prince, and his amity is infinitely more valuable to them than any advantage they could reap by Virginia. . . . Besides I conceive that your followers do not think themselves engaged against the King's authority, but against the Indians."

"But I think otherwise, and am confident of it that it is the mind of this country, and of Maryland, and Carolina also to cast off their governors . . . and if we cannot prevail by arms to make our conditions for peace, or obtain the privilege to elect our own governor, we may retire to Roanoke."

"Sir, the prosecuting what you have discoursed will unavoidably produce utter ruin."

After a pause Bacon asked: "What should a gentleman engaged as I am do? You do as good as tell me I must fly or hang for it."

"I conceive a sensible submission to the Assembly. . . ."

So Goode left him to think over the various steps which had led him on to his present desperate situation. But he did not take the advice to submit. That would mean deserting the people before their wrongs had been righted, it would mean going back to the old despotism with all its injustices and oppressions. He would rather take his chances of defeating the King's troops, confederating with other colonies, and securing the aid of one or more of England's enemy nations. Desperate though these plans seemed, it is possible that they might have succeeded, had not an untimely death overtaken him. Holland, with bitter recollections of two recent wars with England, might have welcomed a chance to break up the British Empire and regain her lucrative tobacco trade. In its essential points it was the same plan which brought independence to America a century later almost to a day.

While Bacon was dreaming of a complete break with England his father was pleading with the King to pardon him. His only son had been unhappily prevailed upon by the importunity of his distressed neighbors to lead them forth against the cruel and perfidious enemies, the Indians. In this way he had "become obnoxious to the letter of the law."

With his petition Thomas Bacon presented an appeal from his son's followers called "The Virginians' Plea." They were in danger day and night, especially those who lived dispersedly on the frontier, from the murderous Indians, and many had been

35

forced to desert their plantations. So they offered their services to go out against them, "having still so much English blood in us . . . as to risk our lives in opposing them . . . rather than to be sneakingly murdered in our beds. . . . Oh Heavens! what a sad dilemma! We confess we have vented our discontents in complaints of other grievances also, too great to be wholly smothered." But they had taken up arms not to relieve themselves by the sword from them, since they thought it better to wait patiently until they could appeal to the King, the governor, the Assembly, and Parliament.

But the period of patient waiting was now at an end. Bacon and his men were in possession of all Virginia west of the Chesapeake Bay. The immediate question was how to defend it against the governor and perhaps an expedition from England. For this the control of the water was vital. The four great rivers gave easy access to the heart of the colony to an enemy fleet, but were serious obstacles to moving troops by land. Without war vessels it would be necessary for Bacon to divide his little army into numerous widely separated detachments in order to defend hundreds of miles of shore.

Lying in the James River were three merchantmen, the *Honour and Dorothy*, the *Rebecca*, commanded by Captain Larrimore, and another *Rebecca*, commanded by Captain Eveling. On August 1 Giles Bland and William Carver, the latter "an able mariner and soldier," rowed out to Larrimore's ship, and though fired on, captured her. They then drew her up at Jamestown and mounted several guns on her from the fort. In the meanwhile Bacon, thinking Berkeley might be aboard Eveling's vessel, demanded permission to search her. But Eveling refused, calling him a rebel and naming him "Oliver Bacon", and before Larrimore's vessel could attack him, weighed anchor, slipped down the river, and headed for England.

Though disappointed at Eveling's escape Bland and Carver, with the *Rebecca*, a small bark, and a sloop, carrying a force of two hundred and fifty men, stationed themselves at the mouth of the James, ready to seize and to press into service any incoming vessels. But they made the mistake of moving across the bay and anchoring off Accomac to treat with the governor. Carver, with 160 men, came ashore in a pinnace. Berkeley tried to persuade him to desert Bacon, but he replied that "if he served the devil he would be true to his trust."

Berkeley ordered him to be gone within eight hours, but contrary winds sprang up so that he had to delay. This Berkeley thought Carver was glad of, since it gave him an opportunity to wean his soldiers away from him. But it proved a godsend for Berkeley. At about midnight a message came to him from Captain Larrimore, explaining that he and his crew served under duress, that there were only forty soldiers left on board the *Rebecca*, and that if he could send thirty or forty gentlemen to the ship, he was sure they, with the help of the sailors, could retake her.

So Philip Ludwell with two boats went out under cover of darkness. As they approached the ship the soldiers on deck hesitated to fire on them, thinking they were coming at Carver's invitation. So they drew up alongside and clambered in through the gunroom ports. As they rushed up on deck they were joined by the sailors with handspikes, and together they soon forced the soldiers to surrender. In the meanwhile Carver too was approaching, and hearing the shouts, tried to veer away. But Larrimore trained his guns on him and captured him and all his men. Coming on board he "stormed, tore his hair off and cursed," as well he might for he knew that he would soon be on the way to the gallows. This was a major victory, for it gave the governor control of the water. From now on he was safe from any attempt to invade the Eastern Shore. On the other hand, he could at will strike at any point up the great Virginia rivers.

While these events were taking place Bacon was leading an army through the woods and swamps of upper Gloucester and Middlesex. He had good reason to believe that it was the Pamunkeys who had made some recent incursions, and he was determined to ferret them out. But it proved a difficult task. His men, tired of wandering here and there, soaked by drenching rains, and half-starved, began to waver. But their dauntless young leader, after permitting many to return, resumed the search with the rest.

They had gone but a few miles when they came upon an Indian village, protected on three sides by swamps, and on the other by thickets and bushes. As the English charged the terrified Indians fled. Many were shot down, many others captured. The queen of the Pamunkeys escaped, and wandered through the woods for days, half starved. Bacon led his men back in triumph, bringing forty-five prisoners, and stores of wampum, skins, furs, and English goods.

But having broken the power of the Pamunkeys, Bacon had now to meet forces raised by the governor. Soon after the capture of the *Rebecca* Captain Gardiner joined the little fleet with the *Adam and Eve*. So Berkeley, embarking 200 men on the ships and on six or seven sloops, crossed over to the Western Shore where another hundred joined them. Then they sailed up the James to Jamestown. Bacon's garrison, perhaps fearing the guns on the ships and thinking themselves outnumbered, fled in the night without firing a shot.

Bacon received this news calmly, though Berkeley declared that "he swore one thousand of his usual execrable oaths." At the time he had but one hundred and thirty-six tired and hungry men with him. But he was determined to lead them to the attack. "Gentlemen and fellow soldiers, how am I transported with gladness to find you thus unanimous, bold and daring, brave and gallant!" he said. "You have the victory before you fight, the conquest before the battle. . . . I know you have the prayers and well-wishes of all the people of Virginia, while the others are loaded with their curses."

Of this they had abundant evidence, for as they trudged along the people brought out "fruits and victuals," shouted encouragement, and denounced the governor. There was a brief stop in New Kent while recruits came in, before they set off for James City County. There the youthful leader delivered another address to his men: "If ever you have fought well and bravely, you must do so now. . . . They call us rebels and traitors, but we will see whether their courage is as great as their pretended loyalty. Come on, my hearts of gold, he who dies in the field of battle dies in the bed of honor."

When Bacon arrived before Jamestown the place seemed impregnable. The narrow isthmus which was the only approach to the town was defended by three heavy guns, the ships in the river were ready to give support, the Back Creek and a series of marshes protected the north shore. But Bacon was not discouraged. All night long his men labored to throw up a makeshift fortress of "trees, bush and earth" facing the isthmus, as a protection should Berkeley's force sally out. When the governor saw what was going on he ordered the ships and shallops to move up to fire on the crude structure, while his soldiers let loose with repeated volleys. Thereupon Bacon sent out parties of horse through the adjacent plantations to bring in the wives of some of the governor's supporters, Elizabeth Page, Angelica Bray, Anna Ballard, Frances Thorpe and even Elizabeth Bacon, wife of his cousin, Nathaniel Bacon, Senior. The terrified ladies were placed upon the ramparts, where they would be in great peril should the firing be resumed, and kept there until Bacon had completed the work and mounted his guns.

It was on September 15, that Berkeley's troops sallied out, formed in front of Bacon's fort, and rushed forward, horse and foot "pressing very close upon one another's shoulders." They made an excellent target, so that when the rebels opened on them, those in front threw down their arms and fled. Had Bacon pressed close on their heels he might have taken the place, and with it Berkeley, and all his men. But he held back and the opportunity was lost.

The governor was furious, and reviled his officers in "passionate terms." But it should have been obvious to him that he could not trust men who fought under compulsion, many of them in sympathy with Bacon. "The common soldiers mutinied, and the officers did not do their whole duty to suppress them," he wrote afterwards. The officers urged on him the necessity of abandoning the town. "One night having rode from guard to guard and from quarter to quarter all day long to encourage the men, I went to bed," Berkeley said. "I was no sooner lain down but there came three or four of the chief officers and told me I must presently rise and go to the ships for the soldiers were all mutinying . . . and that 200 or 300 men were landed at the back of us." But when he put on his clothes, mounted his horse, and rode to the spot they had indicated, he found the report false.

The next day the officers again urged the evacuation of the place. But the governor demurred, "desiring them with all passionate earnestness to keep the town . . . I told them I could neither answer this to the King nor to any man that ever was a soldier, unless they gave under their hands the necessity of my dishonorable quitting the place." This they immediately did and then hurried him away to the fleet. That night guns were spiked, arms and stores were taken on board the vessels, and the soldiers were embarked. Then silently the little fleet slipped down the river.

The next morning Bacon's men occupied the town. But now he was uncertain as to what he should do with it. News had come that Giles Brent, a former supporter of Bacon who had gone over to the governor, had raised an army in the northern counties and was marching south to attack him. Brent, who was half Indian, was a sacrilegious man who was said to have drunk the devil's health, at the same time firing his pistol "to give the devil a gun." His advance put Bacon in a quandary. If he remained in Jamestown, he would be trapped between Brent on land and Berkeley's fleet by water. If he deserted the town, Berkeley would return and occupy it. In the end, he, Lawrence, Drummond, and the others decided to burn the town.

A few minutes later the village was a mass of flames. Lawrence applied the torch to his own house, Drummond to his, and Bacon to the church. They "burnt five houses of mine," reported Berkeley, "and twenty of other gentlemen." It was a desperate deed of determined men, a deed which foreshadowed the burning of Norfolk by patriots in the American Revolution a century later to prevent the British from using it as a base of operations.

Turning his back on the ruins of Jamestown, Bacon led his men first to Green Spring, then to the site of Yorktown, and crossing the York River made his headquarters at the residence of Colonel Augustine Warner, in Gloucester. But when word came that Brent's forces were approaching, he wheeled his veterans into line, the "drums thundered out the march," and away they went to meet him. But there was no battle. Brent's men, many of them probably indentured workers who had been forced into service, had no wish to risk their lives for the governor. So, when they heard that Bacon's force was on the march, they refused to fight, deserted their officers, and returned home.

Now that once more Bacon was in possession of all Virginia except the Eastern Shore, his chief concern was the redcoats, whose arrival was reported to be close at hand. Would the people support him in opposing them? So he summoned the Gloucester trained bands and asked them to take an oath to stand by him, fight the English troops, and if they found that they could not defend themselves, their lives, and liberties, to desert the colony.

At this the Gloucester men balked. To fight the King's troops was to defy the might of England. So they asked to be permitted to remain neutral. Deeply disappointed, Bacon reproved them as the worst of sinners who were willing to be saved by others but would not do their part. Then he dismissed them. When he was told that the Reverend James Wadding had tried to dissuade the people from subscribing, he had him arrested. "It is your place to preach in church, not in camps," he said.

Persuasion having failed, Bacon took sterner measures. Setting up a court-martial, he put some of his opponents on trial. But though Berkeley scorned his proposal that they be exchanged for Carver and Bland, none was executed save one deserter. But the trials served their purpose, for when he summoned the militia again they all subscribed to his oath.

Bacon now turned his attention to the Eastern Shore. He realized that so long as Berkeley had there a base of operations, from which he could launch sudden attacks, his position was insecure. So he sent Captain George Farloe, "one of Cromwell's men," with forty soldiers across the bay to surprise and capture Berkeley. But it was not easy to cross so large a body of water in small boats, and Farloe was taken and hanged. Equally futile was a manifesto to the people of the Eastern Shore urging them to rise against the governor.

Bacon gave orders that the estates of the governor and his friends be ransacked for the use of his army, and Green Spring, King's Creek, Warner Hall, and other places, were denuded of their cattle, sheep, hogs, Indian corn, and even blankets and clothing. But when the rough soldiers began to plunder friend and foe alike Bacon called a halt. And instead of hanging every enemy who fell into his hands in retaliation for Berkeley's executions, he released some without bringing them to trial and pardoned others who had been condemned.

To see that his orders were carried out he now planned, probably on the advice of Lawrence and Drummond, to appoint three committees, one "for settling the south side of James River," another to accompany the army "to inquire into the cause of all seizures," and the third to manage the Indian war. To prevent raids by the enemy from the Eastern Shore Bacon ordered the banks of the great rivers "to be guarded all along, to observe their motion, and as they moved to follow them and prevent them from landing or having any provisions sent on board them."

But for the daring young commander the end was at hand. "Before he could arrive at the perfection of his plans providence did that which no other hand durst do." While at his headquarters in the house of Major Thomas Pate, in Gloucester, a few miles east of West Point, he became ill of dysentery. Bacon's enemies accused him of being an atheist, but in his last hours he called in Mr. Wadding to prepare his mind for death. "He died much dissatisfied in mind," we are told, "inquiring ever and anon after the arrival of the frigates and soldiers from England, and asking if the guards were strong about the house." He died October 26, 1676.

Bacon's enemies made much of the fact that he was so infected with lice that his shirts had to be burned, and because of it spoke of his death as infamous. But the lice probably had nothing to do with it, since typhus seems to have been almost unknown in early America. On the other hand, dysentery was fairly common. Bacon's body has never been found. Thomas Mathews tells us that Berkeley wished to hang it on a gibbet, but on exhuming his casket he found in it nothing but stones. It was supposed that the faithful Lawrence, probably in the dark of night, had buried the body in some secret place.

Berkeley gloated over his arch enemy's death. "His usual oath which he swore at least a thousand times a day was 'God damn my blood,'" he wrote, "and God so infected his blood that it bred lice in an incredible number, so that for twenty days he never washed his shirts but burned them. To this God added the bloody flux, and an honest minister wrote this epitaph on him:

'Bacon is dead, I am sorry at my heart
That lice and flux should take the hangman's part'."

But while his enemies scoffed, Bacon's followers mourned. One of them expressed their sorrow and despair in excellent verse:

> "Death why so cruel! What, no other way
> To manifest thy spleene, but thus to slay
> Our hopes of safety, liberty, our all
> Which, through thy tyranny, with him must fall
> To its late chaos? Had thy rigid force
> Been dealt by retail, and not thus in gross,
> Grief had been silent: Now we must complain
> Since thou, in him, hast more than thousand slain . . ."

What, we may ask, should be Bacon's place in history? Is he to be looked upon only as a rash young man, whose ambition and insistence on having his own way brought disaster to the colony and death to many brave men? Or should he be regarded as a martyr to the cause of liberty? That Bacon was precipitate, that his judgement was faulty at times there can be no doubt. But that he fought to put an end to Berkeley's "French despotism", to restore true representative government in the colony, to break the power of the group of parasites who surrounded the governor, to end unjust and excessive taxes, to make local government more democratic, is obvious. He said so repeatedly. When Bacon and his men said they had enough English blood in their veins not to be murdered in their beds by the Indians, they might have added that they had enough English blood not to remain passive while a despotic old governor robbed them of their liberty. When Bacon's enemies tried to cast opprobrium upon him by calling him the Oliver Cromwell of Virginia, they did not realize that future generations would consider this an unintentional tribute. Certainly he must have been a man of great magnetism, power of persuasion, and sincerity, a man who had a cause to plead, who could arouse the

SIR WILLIAM BERKELEY
From the Original Portrait by an Unknown Artist, now in the possession
of Maurice du Pont Lee, Greenwich, Connecticut.
Canvas measures 49½ x 40½ inches.

From Alexander W. Weddell, Virginia Historical Portraiture.
Courtesy Virginia State Chamber of Commerce

Bacon's Castle

Photo by Flournoy, Virginia State Chamber of Commerce

devotion of so many thousands. But it was true, as one sorrowing follower wrote, that

> "none shall dare his obsequies to sing
> In deserv'd measures, until time shall bring
> Truth crown'd with freedom, and from danger free,
> To sound his praises to posterity."

Bacon's death left the rebels without a leader. Berkeley stated that they would have made Bland their general had he not been his prisoner. What was needed was a man with experience in both military and governmental affairs. Had either Lawrence or Drummond been soldiers one or the other might have been chosen, but apparently neither had ever borne arms. So the army elected Joseph Ingram, who had been second in command under Bacon. Colonel Nicholas Spencer called him "a debauched young man, who this year came to Virginia, and said to be a saddler in England."

Ingram never had the full confidence of his men. He seems to have had some ability as a general, but he was unequal to the task of maintaining order and uniting the distracted colony. Berkeley said that he continued the other officers, but that they "soon disagreed amongst themselves, mistrusting each other."

His task was difficult. If he divided his forces to protect every exposed place along the river banks they might be overwhelmed one by one. It might have been wise for him to carry out Bacon's plan for a flying body of cavalry centered at West Point, within striking distance of the south bank of the Rappahannock, both banks of the York, and the north bank of the James. This would not have prevented night raids by Berkeley's men, but it would have protected the heart of the colony from serious invasion. But Ingram was faced with the problem of feeding his men. The rivers had always been the chief means of communication, but now barges or sloops bringing grain or meat might be intercepted by the *Adam and Eve*, or the *Rebecca*, or the newly arrived warship, the *Concord*. And there was a limit to what could be had by plundering the neighboring plantations.

So Ingram adopted the plan of keeping his main force at the head of the York, and establishing small garrisons at selected points. On the south side of the James he posted a "considerable number" of resolute men in the residence of Major Arthur Allen, known today as Bacon's Castle. At the governor's residence at Green Spring he left about one hundred men under Captain Drew, who guarded the north bank of the James and made away with what was left of Berkeley's cattle, sheep, and grain.

On the south side of the York Major Thomas Whaley, "a stout ignorant fellow", was in command at King's Creek, the estate of Councillor Bacon, while lower down Captain Thomas Hansford, a man of the highest character, was stationed at the site of Yorktown. Across the river another group fortified Mr. William Howard's house, while in Westmoreland still another made their headquarters at the residence of Colonel John Washington.

Hansford, Whaley, Gregory Wakelett, and other officers were men of ability, who could be trusted to remain firm in the cause for which they took up arms. But after Bacon's death the rank and file were filled up partly with slaves and indentured workers, who had little interest in either the Indian war or in curbing the governor's despotism. The garrison at Colonel West's house, near West Point, consisted of about 400 men, of whom eighty were Negroes, and many others were servants. What they wanted was their freedom. But among them there must have been some of Bacon's veterans, for they continued to fight well.

But now the policy of dividing the army into isolated garrisons began to bear bitter fruit. In November, Major Robert Beverley crossed the bay with a strong force in a fleet of transports, entered the York river, and surprised the men at the site of Yorktown. Hansford was captured. A few days later Beverley returned to the York and after a brief encounter captured Major Edmund Cheeseman and Captain Thomas Wilford.

Berkeley now began a series of executions marked by a brutality unsurpassed in American history. One may excuse the tortures inflicted by the Indians because they were savages. There can be no excuse for an Englishman of culture and gentle birth. Extremely avaricious, he had seen the accumulation of a lifetime taken from him; proud of his ability as a ruler, he had seen his government overthrown and had been forced to take refuge in an inaccessible corner of the colony; revering, almost idolizing, the King, he must now explain to him his failures. So his vindictiveness against the men he held responsible knew no bounds.

His first victim was Hansford. When he was condemned by Berkeley's council of war, he pleaded that he might be shot like a soldier not hanged like a dog. "But you are not condemned as a soldier, but as a rebel taken in arms," he was told. As he stood on the scaffold he spoke to the crowd, protesting "that he died a loyal subject and a lover of his country."

When Major Cheeseman was brought in, Berkeley sternly asked him why he had joined the rebels. But as he was about to reply his wife rushed in and told the governor that it was she who had urged him to take up arms, and pleaded that she might be hanged in his place. Though the governor knew that what she said "was near the truth," he spurned her with a vile insult. Yet he was cheated of his revenge, for Cheeseman died in prison, and so escaped the ignominy of the gallows.

When Farloe was brought to trial he pointed out that he held a commission to serve under Bacon signed by Berkeley himself. But this did not save him. The court told him he had been authorized only to fight the Indians, not to take up arms against the governor. "Be silent, while sentence is pronounced on you." The executions of Hansford, Carver, Farloe, Wilford, and John Johnson, "a stirrer up of the people but no fighter," brought to an end the hangings on the Eastern Shore.

Word now reached Berkeley that Major Lawrence Smith had raised the loyal standard in Gloucester, and had assembled a force so large that they could have "beaten all the rebels in the country only with their axes and hoes." In nearby Middlesex another large force was ready to cooperate with him. This seemed the opportunity to crush the rebellion. So the governor embarked 100 men on four ships and several sloops and entered the York river to close in on Ingram from the south while the others attacked from the north and east. But the plan failed miserably.

Ingram met the Middlesex threat by sending Gregory Wakelett out with a body of horse. But when he arrived he found that the enemy had dispersed. Nor were Smith's loyalists more resolute. As they faced Ingram's force a certain Major Bristow stepped out of the ranks and offered to try the justice of the governor's cause after the manner of the Middle Ages by single combat. Ingram himself would have accepted the challenge, but his men caught him by the arm and pulled him back. As it turned out there was no battle, for the rank and file of the so-called loyal forces tamely laid down their arms and went home.

A raid on the right bank of the York also ended in failure. Berkeley decided to send Captain Hubert Farrill with a strong force to surprise the garrison at King's Creek. It was planned to drive in the sentries and to "enter pell mell with them into the house." But they were met by such a deadly fire that they fell back under the shelter of the outbuildings, and then fled to their boats. Farrill was left dead, his commission "dropping wet with blood in his pocket."

But the colony was now in a deplorable condition. Many plantations had been deserted, others had been plundered by the rebels, Ingram had not been able to keep order, there was no money to meet governmental expenses, the desertion of servants and slaves to the rebels, and the absence from the fields of so many small farmers had caused a shortage of the tobacco and corn crops, many houses had been burned, the courts in some of the counties were closed. The rebel officers could not restrain their rough soldiers from wanton destruction—throwing down fences, destroying crops, burning barns. Soon the longing for peace and order became general. Time was working for the governor.

However, it was known that Colonel Herbert Jeffreys with 1000 men had been ordered to go to Virginia to suppress the rebellion, and their arrival was expected at any moment.

In the meanwhile the tobacco ships began to come in with needed supplies of clothing, cloth, medicines, etc. The planters still had some hogsheads of tobacco on hand, and were anxious to resume trade with the merchants, but when Berkeley issued a proclamation threatening to denounce as a rebel anyone who traded with the Western Shore the shippers held back. So the planters realized that the weapon of economic pressure, of which Goode had warned Bacon, was to be applied against them.

And they must have been discouraged when, in November, the ship *Concord* of 500 tons, armed with 30 guns and commanded by Thomas Grantham, entered through the capes and anchored in the York river. Lawrence wrote Grantham a letter telling him that the people had been grievously oppressed and begging him and the merchants to remain neutral. Otherwise they were determined to burn their tobacco. Grantham replied that he would not treat with men who had taken up arms against the royal authority.

But he did offer his services to effect a reconciliation. Sending a boat for Berkeley, he received him on board the *Concord*, where he tried to persuade him "to meekness," pointing out that an unrelenting temper would only drive the rebels to a desperate resistance. Meekness was something far from Berkeley's heart, but he was desperately anxious to end the rebellion before the redcoats arrived. Then he could tell the King that he, unassisted, had restored order. To accomplish this he was even willing to forego the satisfaction of hanging some of the leaders of the rebellion, provided Lawrence and Drummond were not among them.

So he sent Grantham up the river to the Pate house, where he found Ingram with about 800 men. After prolonged negotiations Ingram yielded and surrendered West Point together with 300 men, four great guns, and many small arms.

Grantham then went to Colonel John West's house, where he found a garrison of about 400 English and Negroes. They accused him of betraying them, and some were for shooting him, others for cutting him in pieces. But after he had put them in better humor with a barrel of brandy they "surrendered the post, with three cannon, 500 muskets and fowling pieces, and 1000 pounds of bullets."

Grantham now delivered Ingram, Colonel Langston, and other rebel officers to Berkeley, who at once pardoned them. He next went to Ingram's house, marched the garrison there down to Tindall's Point, took their arms, drums, and colors, and gave them the oath of allegiance. After the men had toasted the King and the governor, they gave three shouts and dispersed. We may judge the extent of Berkeley's elation at the collapse of the rebellion by the fact that he invited Ingram and Langston to dine with him on shipboard.

But Gregory Wakelett, one of the most active of the rebel leaders, was still at large with a force of cavalry. So anxious was Berkeley to secure his submission that he promised him, not only his pardon, but part of the wampum his men had taken from the Indians. So he too "declared for the King." When other posts on the James and the York were surrendered or abandoned, Lawrence, Drummond, and Whaley, with a force of several hundred men, were all that were left of the rebel army. They well knew that for them there would be no mercy. But as they retreated into New Kent their men began to fall off until they were entirely deserted.

Lawrence and Whaley with three others determined to risk

torture at the hands of the Indians rather than fall into the hands of the governor. They were last seen on the extreme frontier, pushing on through the snow into the forest. We shall probably never know their fate. They may have died of hunger and exposure, they may have been killed by the Indians; it is barely possible that they found refuge in one of the northern colonies. But though the fate of Lawrence and Whaley is shrouded in mystery, that of many others is known. The enraged governor drew up a long list of those he had marked for the gallows. When the reports of Berkeley's savagery reached Charles II, he is said to have remarked "That old fool has hanged more men in that naked country than I have for the murder of my father."

Drummond was found hiding in Chickahominy Swamp and brought before the governor at King's Creek. The vindictive old man made a low bow, saying, "Mr. Drummond, you are very welcome. I am more glad to see you than any man in Virginia. Mr. Drummond, you shall be hanged in half an hour." However, he decided to give him at least the pretence of a trial. But his ring was snatched from his finger, his clothes taken from his back, and he was kept overnight in irons. The next morning he was forced to walk, still in irons, in bitterly cold weather, all the way to Middle Plantation. There, after a brief hearing, in which he was not allowed to defend himself, he was hurried away to the scaffold. His widow and five children were driven out of their house and forced to flee into the woods and swamps, where they came near starvation.

When Anthony Arnold, who was one of the sturdiest supporters of the rebellion, was brought into court, he boldly defended the right of the people to resist oppression. "It is well known that I have no kindness for Kings," he told the court. "They have no rights but what they got by conquest and the sword, and he that can by force of the sword deprive them of it has as good and just a title to it as the King himself. If the King should deny to do me right I would make no more to sheathe my sword in his heart or bowels than of my mortal enemies." The court was sorry that the country was not "capable of executing the sentence peculiar to traitors according to the laws and custom of England." This was to hang the victim for several minutes, cut him down when still alive, rip him open, cut off his head, and then quarter him. So they contented themselves with hanging him in chains, "to be a more remarkable example than the rest."

The executions continued for several months. Thomas Young, James Wilson, Henry Page, and Thomas Hall were executed on January 12, 1677; William Drummond and John Baptista on January 20; James Crews, William Cookson, and John Digbie on January 24; Giles Bland and Anthony Arnold on March 8; John Isles and Richard Pomfrey on March 15; and John Whitson and William Scarburgh on March 16. There is no telling how many Berkeley might have hanged had not the Assembly asked him to stop.

The people were deeply angered at the governor's brutality. Governor Notley thought that "were there any person bold and courageous in Virginia that dared venture his neck, the commons of Virginia would enmire themselves as deep in rebellion as ever they did in Bacon's time." And for months in hundreds of humble cottages men were on the lookout for the return of Lawrence, ready to seize their arms and follow him in a new uprising.

There was no hope of relief from the new Assembly which met at Green Spring, February 20, 1677. William Sherwood said that most of the Burgesses were the governor's "own creatures and chose by his appointments." Jeffreys testified that they had been "not so legally nor freely chosen," and that the "Council, Assembly, and people" were "overawed" by Berkeley. That Berkeley allowed such an Assembly to re-enact in substantially the same form several of Bacon's laws, shows that he was not entirely deaf to the rumblings of a new rebellion.

In the meanwhile King Charles had appointed Colonel Herbert Jeffreys, Sir John Berry, and Colonel Francis Moryson commissioners to go to Virginia to inquire into the people's grievances. At the same time he ordered Berkeley to return to England "with all possible speed." During his absence Jeffreys was to act in his place with the title of Lieutenant Governor. With them came the redcoats.

No sooner had the commissioners arrived than Berkeley became involved in a bitter quarrel with them. When they told him to obey the King's orders to come to England, he made excuses to linger until he had taken his revenge on the rebels. Jeffreys brought with him a proclamation pardoning all the rebels with the sole exception of Bacon, but when Berkeley published it he had the audacity to exempt from it not only two men who had died during the war, fourteen who had already been executed, and twenty-six others whom he mentioned by name, but all those "now in prison for rebellion or under bond for the same." Of those in prison and not mentioned by name in the proclamation Robert Stoakes, John Isles, Richard Pomfrey, John Whitson, and William Scarburgh were later executed.

Berkeley was also determined to make good his personal losses from the estates of the rebels. "I have lost at least £8000 sterling in houses, goods, plantation, servants, and cattle, and never expect to be restored to a quarter of it," he complained. The rebels left "me not one grain of corn, not one cow . . . I have not £5 in the world." So he, Beverley, Philip Ludwell, and others of the "loyal party," were furious when Jeffreys insisted that they stop breaking open and plundering the houses and barns of the former rebels, and take their complaints to the courts.

For three months Berkeley postponed his departure, but at last, on April 25, he went on board the *Rebecca*, the vessel which had been of such vital importance to him during the rebellion, and set sail for England. But he was now a very ill man. "He came here alive but . . . unlike to live," wrote Secretary Coventry. He died on July 13, 1677, and was interred at Twickenham.

With the death of Berkeley a main cause of discontent and insubordination in Virginia was removed. Though Culpeper and Effingham, who succeeded in turn to the governorship, made onslaughts on the liberties of the people, they acted, not from any overwhelming desire to make themselves absolute, but because they reflected the spirit of the Second Stuart Despotism. But this came to an end with the Glorious Revolution of 1688-89, and from that time to the passage of the Stamp Act, the people of Virginia had no need to take arms to defend their liberties. For decades after Bacon's Rebellion, the King and the governors were wary of bearing down upon them too hard for fear of causing another uprising. For the time they had learned their lesson. And had they not forgotten it after the lapse of a century, there might have been no American Revolution.

When one reviews the tragic events in Virginia during the fateful year of 1676, one may well ask: "Would the rebellion have occurred had there been no Indian war?" Possibly not. Berkeley was aging and within a few years he might have died, and a less despotic governor taken his place. Had the planters waited, their lot would have been bettered by the rising price of tobacco. On the other hand, it is possible that if the war had not touched off the rebellion something else would have done so.

Would the Indian war have started the rebellion had the mass of the people had no other grievances? This seems unlikely. When the news of the uprising reached Charles II he thought it past belief that "so considerable a body of men, without the least grievance or oppression, should rise up in arms and overturn the government." And so it would have been past belief had there been no grievance or oppression.

Had the dispute between Bacon and Berkeley as to how the war should be conducted been all there was at issue, the people would hardly have risen in wild anger to overthrow the government, drive the governor into exile, defy the King, make ready to resist his forces, and risk death on the gallows. Philip Ludwell said that the rebel army was made up of men "whose condition . . . was such that a change could not make worse." Had not the English trade laws, misgovernment, and injustice practically eliminated the middle class there would have been hundreds to whom the maintaining of law and order was the first consideration. They would have supported Berkeley's Indian policy, however unwise, rather than risk their estates. As it was, the governor found himself practically deserted. Never before was there "so great a madness as this base people are generally seized with," he complained.

No one will contend that the firing on Fort Sumter was the cause of the War between the States, or that the murder of the Archduke Ferdinand was the cause of the first World War. These were but the matches thrown into the powder kegs. The kegs had been filling up for many years, and sooner or later explosions were inevitable. So in Virginia had there been no powder keg, the lighted match of the Indian war would probably have flickered and burnt itself out.

In most great upheavals men have mixed motives. Of course Bacon and his men rose in arms partly to protect themselves and their families from the Indians. They said so repeatedly. But we have abundant evidence from both sides that they were determined also to put an end to oppression and misgovernment. "As for Bacon's designs of prosecuting the Indian war it is most evident that he never intended anything more in it than a covert under which to act all his villanies," wrote Philip Ludwell. "If these had not been the chief motives they had certainly understanding enough to have led them a fairer way to presenting their grievances than on their swords' points."

The Council, in a long statement, written when the uprising was but a few weeks old, declared that Bacon's "only aim has always been and is nothing else but of total subversion of the government." Thomas Ludwell and Robert Smith, who at the time were in England, on receiving reports of the rebellion, said that when the Indian raids began "some idle and poor people made use of the present conjunction for their ill designs." William Sherwood, an eyewitness of what took place, testified that "it is most true that the great oppressions and abuses of the people by the governor's arbitrary will hath been the cause of the late troubles there." Colonel Jeffreys, who was commissioned by the King to investigate the causes of the uprising, put the blame, not on the Indian war, but upon Philip Ludwell and Robert Beverley, who "were the great advisors of Berkeley, and as it may be proved were the chief causes of the miseries that befell the country in the rebellion."

Governor Notley, of Maryland, stated that "whatever palliations the great men of Virginia may use at the Council board in England . . . yet you may be sure . . . much . . . if not every tittle of the accusations against them is truth." If the new governor, Colonel Herbert Jeffreys should "build his proceedings upon the old foundation, 'tis neither him nor all his Majesty's soldiers in Virginia will either satisfy or rule those people. They have been strangely dealt with by their former magistracy." Just two days later Nicholas Spencer wrote that though the rebellion was over, "the putrid humors of our unruly inhabitants are not so allayed but that they do frequently vent themselves . . . and were they not awed by the overruling hand of his Majesty would soon express themselves by violent acts."

As for Bacon, he had been in command of the frontier forces but a few days when he sent messengers to every part of the colony to blast Berkeley's misgovernment. The Council reported to the Board of Trade that he had traduced the governor "with many false and scandalous charges." Later, in manifesto after manifesto, Bacon assailed the corruption, the inefficiency, and the injustices of Berkeley's regime. "We appeal to the country itself what and of what nature their oppressions have been, and by what cabals . . . carried on." By taking on himself "the sole nominating" of civil and military officers he had made himself master of the colony. He had permitted his favorites "to lay and impose what levies and impositions upon us they should or did please, which they for the most part converted to their own private lucre and gain." As for seeking relief by petitioning the Burgesses, he said: "Consider what hope there is of redress in appealing to the very persons our complaints do accuse."

Thomas Mathews tells us that it was "the received opinion in Virginia" that the Indian war was the excuse for Bacon's Rebellion rather than the cause. Since Mathews took part in the uprising and later wrote an account of it, he should know. He even goes so far as to say that it was Thomas Lawrence, not Bacon, who was chiefly responsible for the uprising. Bacon "was too young," he points out, "too much a stranger there, and of a disposition too precipitate to manage things to that length they were carried, had not thoughtful Mr. Lawrence been at the bottom."

This man had his personal grievance, Mathews states, for he had been cheated out of a "considerable estate on behalf of a corrupt favorite." His wife kept a tavern at Jamestown, which gave him an opportunity to meet persons from all parts of the colony. So he filled their ears with complaints of the governor. Mathews himself had heard him suggest "some expedient not only to repair his great loss, but therewith to see those abuses rectified that the country was oppressed with through . . . the forwardness, avarice, and French despotic methods of the governor." As for Bacon and his adherents, they "were esteemed as but wheels agitated by the weight" of Lawrence's resentments, after their rage had been raised to a high pitch by Berkeley's failure to put a stop to the effusions of blood by the Indians.

Lawrence had the hearty support of William Drummond, a Scotsman who also resided in Jamestown. Like Lawrence he had a grievance against Berkeley. In fact the governor was inclined to believe that he had been "the original cause of the whole rebellion." We know that Lawrence and Drummond stood at Bacon's elbow from the beginning to the end. The importance of the part they played may be gauged by the bitterness of Berkeley's resentment. "I so hate Drummond and Lawrence that though they could put the country in peace in my hands, I would not accept it from such villains," he declared.

But whatever was the role of these two men, whatever the part played by Bacon, the rebellion is a landmark in the development of self-government in Virginia. Though Bacon met an untimely death, though Drummond was led to the gallows, though Lawrence disappeared in the icy forest, their efforts were not in vain. They, and the thousands who supported them, had taught future governors that there was a limit to oppression beyond which they dare not go. The roar of their cannon proclaimed to the world that Virginians would resist to the end all attempts to deprive them of their heritage of English liberty.

ESSAY ON AUTHORITIES

The opening to investigators of the Marquess of Bath Papers by the British Manuscripts Project has thrown new light on Bacon's Rebellion. There are several letters from Bacon to Berkeley and several from Berkeley to Bacon. They show that Berkeley went to England during the Civil War to fight for the King, that Bacon was related to Lady Berkeley, that Lady Berkeley was in England during most of the rebellion, and that she corresponded with Philip Ludwell.

The Bath Papers add to the already abundant evidence that Bacon fought partly to end misgovernment in Virginia. The evidence comes not only from Bacon's supporters but from Berkeley himself, Ludwell, and others.

Berkeley's letters explain why he did not hang Bacon when he had him in his power, why he dissolved the Long Assembly and called for a new election based on a widened franchise, why he evacuated the almost impregnable post of Jamestown. There are several revealing letters by Philip Ludwell.

Historians have long been acquainted with the county grievances collected by the King's commissioners. They are to be found in the British Public Record Office, CO5-1371, have now been transcribed by the Library of Congress and some have been published in the *Virginia Magazine*, Vols. II and III. The most detailed and probably the least prejudiced account of the rebellion is the *True Narrative of the Rise, Progress and Cessation of the Late Rebellion in Virginia*, by the commissioners. The only narrative we have of the transactions of the Assembly of June, 1676, by one of the members is Thomas Mathews' *The Beginning, Progress and Conclusion of Bacon's Rebellion*, published in C. M. Andrews' *Narratives of Insurrections* and elsewhere. Important also are *Bacon's Proceedings* and *Ingram's Proceedings*, attributed to Mrs. Ann Cotton. Bacon's expedition to the Roanoke river, the defeat of the Susquehannocks, and the battle on Occaneechee Island are described in a document entitled "A Description of the Fight between the English and the Indians in May, 1676," published in the *William and Mary Quarterly*, Series 1, Vol. IX, pp. 1-4. The account given by the Council is in the Bath Papers.

W. W. Hening's *Virginia Statutes at Large* is a storehouse of information. It includes not only the laws of the Restoration period, but many official reports, among them "The Proclamation of Pardon of October 10, 1676," "Bacon's Submission", and the proceedings of some of the courts-martial. The details of the Susquehannock war in Maryland may be pieced together from the accounts by Thomas Mathews, the King's commissioners, Mrs. Cotton, and others. By the aid of an old pen-and-ink

59

diagram of the Susquehannock fort, I have been able to locate the site, and Mrs. Alice L. L. Ferguson to uncover parts of it.

The "Dialogue between John Goode and Nathaniel Bacon," which is in the British Public Record Office, throws light on Bacon's plans to draw North Carolina and Maryland into his rebellion, and to resist the redcoats. Important also are the "Declaration of Thomas Swan and others on August 3, 1676", (GO1-37-42); Philip Ludwell's letters to Lady Berkeley and to Thomas Ludwell, and others (Bath Papers); the "Declaration of the People" (Bath Papers); "Grantham's Account" (Bath Papers); Berkeley's account of the rebellion written on board Sir John Berry's ship, February 2, 1677 (Bath Papers).

Among the secondary sources are Mary Newton Stanard, *The Story of Bacon's Rebellion;* Thomas J. Wertenbaker, *Virginia Under the Stuarts;* and *Torchbearer of the Revolution;* Philip Alexander Bruce, *The Economic History of Virginia in the Seventeenth Century,* and *The Institutional History of Virginia in the Seventeenth Century;* Wesley Frank Craven, *The Southern Colonies in the Seventeenth Century;* John Fiske, *Old Virginia and her Neighbors;* John Burk, *History of Virginia;* Herbert L. Osgood, *The American Colonies in the Seventeenth Century.*

The Virginia Magazine of History and Biography, the *William and Mary Quarterly,* 1st and 2d Series, and *Tyler's Magazine* have printed much material relating to the rebellion, and Dr. E. G. Swem's splendid index covering these volumes has greatly increased their value.

www.ingramcontent.com/pod-product-compliance
Lightning Source LLC
Chambersburg PA
CBHW071230160426
43196CB00012B/2469